Tyrannosaurus Rex

by Charles Lennie

ABDO
DINOSAURS
Kids

www.abdopublishing.com

Published by Abdo Kids, a division of ABDO, PO Box 398166, Minneapolis, Minnesota 55439.

Copyright © 2015 by Abdo Consulting Group, Inc. International copyrights reserved in all countries. No part of this book may be reproduced in any form without written permission from the publisher.

Printed in the United States of America, North Mankato, Minnesota.

052014

092014

Photo Credits: Getty Images, Minnesota Zoo (mnzoo.org), Shutterstock, Thinkstock, © Artush p.cover,5 / Shutterstock, © Matt Martyniuk / CC-BY-3.0 p.19, © A.E. Anderson p.19, © John R. Horner, Mark B. Goodwin, Nathan Myhrvold / CC-BY-2.5 p.19, © Christophe Hendrickx / CC-BY-SA 3.0 p.21

Production Contributors: Teddy Borth, Jennie Forsberg, Grace Hansen

Design Contributors: Candice Keimig, Laura Rask, Dorothy Toth

Library of Congress Control Number: 2013952091

Cataloging-in-Publication Data

Lennie, Charles.

 Tyrannosaurus rex / Charles Lennie.

   p. cm. -- (Dinosaurs)

ISBN 978-1-62970-026-7 (lib. bdg.)

Includes bibliographical references and index.

1. Tyrannosaurus rex--Juvenile literature.   I. Title.

567.912--dc23

                    2013952091

Table of Contents

Tyrannosaurus Rex

The Tyrannosaurus rex lived

a long time ago. It lived about

70 million years ago.

4

The Tyrannosaurus rex made its home near lakes and streams.

The Tyrannosaurus rex
was one of the largest
animals to ever live.

9

The Tyrannosaurus rex was as long as a bus. It was as tall as a giraffe.

The Tyrannosaurus rex stood on two feet. It had two short, strong arms and a very large tail.

The Tyrannosaurus rex had a good sense of smell. It also had great eyesight.

Food

The Tyrannosaurus rex ate meat. It had teeth that were nine inches (23 cm) long!

Fossils

Tyrannosaurus rex fossils have been found throughout North America.

18

Canada

Montana

South
Dakota

Wyoming

Colorado

The most complete
Tyrannosaurus rex **fossil**
ever found is named Sue.
Sue is at a **museum** in
Chicago, Illinois.

More Facts

- The largest Tyrannosaurus rex tooth ever found was 12 inches (30 cm) long!

- If a Tyrannosaurus rex broke a tooth, it could regrow a new tooth.

- Scientists believe the Tyrannosaurus rex could eat 500 pounds (230 kg) of meat in one bite.

- The Tyrannosaurus rex could weigh about 18,000 pounds (8,165 kg). That is more than an elephant.

Glossary

fossils – the remains of a once living thing; could be a footprint or skeleton.

museum – a building that holds and displays valuable and historical objects, like paintings, sculptures, and more.

stream – a flowing body of water; a small river.

Index

abdokids.com

Use this code to log on to abdokids.com and access crafts, games, videos and more!

Abdo Kids Code:

DTK0267

24